Diary of a Poetic Mind

Reflections of Life and Love

Dawn A. Campbell

Order this book online at www.trafford.com/
or email orders@trafford.com

Most Trafford titles are also available at major online book retailers.

Note for Librarians: A cataloguing record for this book is available from Library
and Archives Canada at www.collectionscanada.ca/amicus/index-e.html

Printed in Victoria, BC, Canada.

ISBN: 978-1-4251-8096-6 (sc)

ISBN: 978-1-4251-8796-5 (e-book)

*We at Trafford believe that it is the responsibility of us all, as both individuals
and corporations, to make choices that are environmentally and socially sound.
You, in turn, are supporting this responsible conduct each time you purchase a
Trafford book, or make use of our publishing services. To find out how you are
helping, please visit www.trafford.com/responsiblepublishing.html*

*Our mission is to efficiently provide the world's finest, most comprehensive
book publishing service, enabling every author to experience success.
To find out how to publish your book, your way, and have it available
worldwide, visit us online at www.trafford.com*

www.trafford.com

North America & international
toll-free: 1 888 232 4444 (USA & Canada)
phone: 250 383 6864 ♦ fax: 250 383 6804
email: info@trafford.com

Contents

"I'm thanking you God from a full heart,
I'm writing the book on your wonders.
I'm whistling, laughing, and jumping for joy:
I'm singing your song, high God"
Psalms 9:1-2

Dedicated to Christians and Non-Christians alike. To those who are spirit filled and those who are just filled with the spirit. To believers and non believers alike who decide to follow the road less traveled instead of the road frequently traveled. Those who dare to blaze a trail and start a revolution of the faithfull kind.

Get inspiration, gather life, and continue to drink from the fountain of hope and prosperity, the great book of life. The true foundation of who you are and all and what you can become. Live life, love life and enjoy it to the fullest. Continue to live a blessed life through him.

I hope this book serves as an inspiration to all who is blessed to read it. I hope it gives you as much inspiration to pursue your own goals and true destiny in your life as writing this book has given me.

A special thank you to all my friends and family. Most importantly thank you to all my Devine Connections who have been a tremendous support to me throughout my life. Without their constant support and persuasiveness this book would not have transpired. Thanks to L. Holmes, E. Clayton, E. Watson, A. Franklin and the most important person in my life Mama who is my grandmother Olga Elizabeth Simpson. May God rest her soul.

Once you trust in him and continue to believe in him, all things are possible.
I hope this book helps you all to pursue your life long dream and make it into a reality as I did.

God Bless You All.

Dawn A. Campbell

Diary of a Poetic Mind

Mama

Oh Mama,
I don't want to cry no more.
Visiting your grave,
Brought back great memories.
Times spent together,
Yet apart.
You have never left the crevices of my mind.
You are a constant flow within me,
Giving me sustenance and life,
Just like my heavenly father.

Father God,
Why did she have to go.
Why did she have to leave this earthly place.
I yearn for the days,
When I can see her,
To hold her,
To touch her,
Would be my greatest reward.

Reaching out towards her,
To see her face,
To bless her with life,
Knowing that only you have the power to do so.

Touching her,
Talking to her,
Would be my greatest reward.

Living life,
Loving life.
Having you Olga as a wonderful part of it all.

To sustain life,
Is to retain life,
Maintain life.

To have you,
To hold you,
Having you close to me,
Is a matter of my life,
Remembering the woman that was Olga Elizabeth Simpson.
Rest in Peace oh great one,
Rest in peace,
Until the day of your resurrection,
Everlasting life,
Your greatest reward.

Dawn A. Campbell

Inspirational Quote

Be gracious to me Lord.
For to you I cry all day long.
Make glad the soul of your servant,
For to you, Lord, are good, and ready to forgive,
And abundant in loving kindness to all who call upon you.
Psalms 86:3-5

Falling in and out of love, is not and easy feat. For some it is quite easy to pick yourself up and start all over again. Unfortunately for some, it is not that easy. Too much time is spent blaming one another, and not enough time saying I'm sorry, realizing that you are only human, and as humans we tend to make mistakes. Instead of spending time wallowing in self pity, spend time getting to know yourself. This means knowing who you are and what you want out of life. This way when it is not true love, then you can realize it and be confident enough to move on.

Dawn A. Campbell

Living a Meagre Existence

What kind of world do we live in,
If we keep getting up everyday and argue and fight with one another.
What kind of world do we live in,
With so much racial tension,
Fighting and arguing about the colour of ones skin and the creed of one's kin.
Why can't we all just get along.
We all come from one maker.
We walk the same walk,
Talk the same talk,
We even bleed the same blood.
Can a man change his ways,
Even though he posses the power to choose his own destiny.
Why does such bad blood exist.
In a world rot with degradation, pain and suffering,
Why can't we all just get along.
Accept the faith of what life has dealt us and move on.
Learn to deal with it,
And work towards creating your own destiny,
Since you already have the key.
The key to controlling and operating your very own powerful weapon,
Your mind.
Use it,
Learn from it,
And learn to control it,
In order for it to work properly and effectively for you.

Dawn A. Campbell

Love Gone Astray

In a world full of pain and suffering,
How can we find the perseverance to press on.
How can we continue on knowing that I am in love with you,
And you continue to love another.

How can I get you to notice me,
You seeing only me,
Me seeing you,
While you have eyes for someone else.
Why have you forsaken me.
Why have you turned your back on me.
Once bitten,
Twice shy was the old adage,
Now it's once bitten,
Maybe I should give him another chance.
How many chances do you give,
How many heartache do you have to suffer before the realization hits
you.

How long will you continue,
Prolonging a relationship that is going nowhere.
A relationship that has ended by a party of one,
Not two.

It use to be you and me,
Not you and she.
Now it's just me.
Me with my back pressed against the wall,
Wondering ,
Pondering,
What have I done to deserve this.
Why me and not someone else.

Is it you,
Or me.
Then again will it be me or someone else.
The answer is clear,
Written on the wall,
Etched in stone
You have already chosen,
Made your decision.
It's certainly not me.
Love lost never to be found,
Hoping to be had,
Not today,
But maybe someday.

Dawn A. Campbell

Pain

Where does the hurt go,
Where does the pain go,
When there is love lost,
Between a mother and a daughter.

My how time flies,
When there is no consolation of a love.
To hold,
To capture the essence of love lost,
Stolen,
Taken away before it had a chance to develop.

When do you learn to trust,
To believe in the wondrous powers of a mothers love.

To have,
To hold,
To let go of a love never received,
But yearning to have.

Dawn A. Campbell

The Divorce

Why do you refuse to give me the one thing that means so much to me,
The ultimate D word,
The divorce.
As the relationship sours,
As we drift apart into different directions,
All I want from you to me is a divorce.
No sense in hoping,
Wishing on a love that never was,
Maybe on your part,
But certainly not on mine.
Through the lies,
The deception on your part,
The only conceivable thing to do,
From you to me is to give me the divorce.
No sense in turning back the hands of time.
No sense in wishing anything more than what it really is.
Why is it so difficult for you to commit to the divorce.
Why are you refusing to sign.
Lies and deception your strong forte.
To be deceived by the deceiver is not an easy thing to accept,
But you must in order to move on.
Do I have to pay for it like everything else?
I guess I must,
If I aim to achieve ultimate freedom from you.
What does not kills you makes you stronger.
Strong enough to have the patience and perseverance to wait on the
plans that the heavenly father has in store for you.
When you rise,
He shall go down.
What goes up must come down.
When he is on his down ward spiral,

You shall be lifted up.
God's ultimate plan for you is to prosper you,
Give you hope and a bright future.
Love for him absolutely not.
Divorce from him absolutely yes.

Dawn A. Campbell

The Eyes Have It

Each time I look into those dark relenting eyes,
I am reminded of a love never had,
But hoping desperately to find.

Each time I look in your eyes,
I see the possibility of my one true love,
The one who will love me unconditionally,
The way I want and need to be loved.

Each time I look into your eyes,
I see a shadow of a love,
My one true love that I have searched hard to find,
With never ending failure.

As I look into your eyes,
And you in mine,
What do we see,
But each other.
Two separate but distinct worlds colliding together,
Hoping to find that special love in each other.

Looking into your eyes,
I wonder if I am capable of loving,
Or can I be taught to love again.

If I continue looking into your eyes,
Will I find out that it's a reality and not a dream,
Not a misconception of two lost souls looking for love,
And not finding it in each other.

Dawn A. Campbell

Trials and Tribulation

What to do?
What to do indeed.
What do you do after a love has soured,
Leaving you angry and discontent.
What do you do?
You try to pick up the pieces,
But you just can't seem to pick fast enough,
Cause everything seems to be crumbling around you.
The walls are caving in,
And only you alone know what to do,
But you don't,
Cause you are with child and cannot foresee giving up the child,
Or taking the life of another.
What do you do?
You cry,
You get angry and call each other names.
You act out how you feel,
But that still does not gather a response.
Solutions to the problem comes,
But not without a price.
Answers are not cheap.
Answers,
What are they?
A mere thought or words to soothe a worried or troubled soul.
Somehow there is just no comfort,
No solace for a withering mind.
There is no comfort to relieve all the pain and suffering that has been
done to this withered soul.
Talk is cheap.
The pain keeps on hurting.
There is always a fee involved,
Whether going to the doctors or visiting a friend,

There is a substantial price to be paid when grieving the loss of a love.
Will she loose it,
Will she retain it.
Only she knows,
Or will she ever know.
You tell me,
Tell me,
What's the answer.

Dawn A. Campbell

Unwedded Bliss

You walk down the isle towards what you believe to be your eternal
life.
The words I do is uttered in a moment of love and lust towards a
future,
Yearning for but yet to achieve.
Till death do you part,
Your new slogan towards a blissful life.

How you utter those words joyfully,
Yet years down the road you take them for granted.

Where did the love go,
Was it love or lust.
Was it like or dislike.

Your white dress now marred with the tears running down your
cheeks,
Stunned beyond repair.

Loving you a distant memory,
An ill taste in your mouth.
How you yearn to go back to the way things were,
Before you fell in and out of love,
Trying to salvage a love lost,
Yet to regain.
How could you lie to me,
How could you string me on like a puppet,
Allowing me to believe that,
You I,
We are,
Really in love.

How do you move on from the betrayal,
How do you pick up the pieces and move on.

Lies,
Deception,
To be deceived,
Not seeing the chameleon for who and what he really is.

Hope,
Love and faith,
A living testament to who you are,
And what has gotten you this far.

Hope towards a new life,
Loving yourself and who you have become.
Faith in the eternal father in all and what he has helped you deal with.
Learning to live a faithful life,
A blissful life,
Loving who you are and what you have become.

Dawn A. Campbell

Why Do Bad Things Happen To Good People

In life,
We are faced with unforeseen circumstances,
That we have no control over.

We are treated a certain way,
Looked upon a certain way,
Taken for granted,
And worse of all,
Abused beyond certain control.
Abuse not often seen with the human eye,
Since there is no scar left behind.
All that's left is heavy burdens and crosses to bear.

We are all faced with difficult times,
But never in a million years did you imagine that it would ever get
so bad.

The crosses are becoming taller and the load is getting heavier and
heavier.

When will it ever end,
Will it ever stop.
Your favourite prayer,
Now a séance.
Dear God,
Why me!
Why me!
What have I ever done to deserve this.
Why do bad things happen to good people.
Why do I have to suffer such a silent death.

The pressure is so overwhelming.
Why me and not someone else.
Why me indeed.
The only things I can ask,
Is why do bad things happen to good people.

Dawn A. Campbell

Inspirational Quote

"A new command I give you; love one another
As I have loved you, so you must love one another."
John 13:34

The magic and spirit of love is something that you have to nurture,
take care of and water on a constant and daily basis. Constantly
showing interest and putting interest into the relationship, you will
be surprised how quickly it will grow and blossom in a flower. Take
the time to effectively communicate with one another, loving and
respecting one another and you will see the relationship flourish into
something lasting, exciting and enticing for years to come.

Dawn A. Campbell

A Celebration of Love

Let's celebrate the union of two soul mates united together,
Divided they will not fall.
A single unit,
Tied together by a circular band,
Mumbling,
Uttering the words I do,
Until death do they part.

Let's celebrate the union of an elegant couple.
One in love with name brands,
The other loving the brand of the name,
Adoring and loving his mate.
A vibrant couple,
Living a wonderful life,
A fabulous life,
A blessed life together.

Let's give a toast of good cheer,
To the couple of the year,
Loving life,
Living life,
Being very much in love with each other.

Let's give a toast to a sanctified union,
A concreted union made for two.
Made by man,
Developed by God,
Loving them,
Serving them and taking care of them to the very end.

Blessed are those who walk in the shadow of the almighty,
They will live a long and prosperous life.

Dawn A. Campbell

Chameleon
Deceive the Deceiver

Beautiful you are to me.
Beauty is in the eye of the beholder.
One persons good,
Is another persons bad.
What is good to me,
May not be to you.

How beautiful are you,
Depends on the individual.
To look at another with deceptive eyes,
Is to look upon the face of a deceiver.

Like a chameleon,
They come in all shapes,
Sizes and color.
To create a story,
Believable by all,
To not let known the true purpose of the mission.

Believable but true,
I have been deceived by you.

Feeling hurt,
Feeling pain,
At the situation I have found myself in not knowing where to turn,
where to go.
I have fallen deep into his deceptive trap.

Lying,
Scheming,

Diary of a Poetic Mind

To achieve your own material gain.
I have fought a good fight,
Went to war,
And have lost the battle.

No more tears will I shed.
No more blood will I bleed.
I have seen that side of you,
Unseen by most human.

Your agenda is now known,
Your case now spoken,

Pleading your case for all to hear,
Hoping to see the results of your material gain.

Love spawn,
Had,
But lost.
Spurn to turn the tide,
Towards the next victim.
I have lost now,
But just remember who laughs last,
Laughs the best.
When my rewards have come,
Yours have fallen.
Fallen into the inevitable abyss of the deceptive trap.

Dawn A. Campbell

Communication

Communication,
Open to discuss,
Fleeing words,
Yearning to burst forth from within.
Words spoken by many,
Never amounting to anything.
Motivating,
Uplifting,
Inspiring,
Never allowed to blossom,
To flourished,
Yearning to break free.
To communicate,
To listen,
To reflect on words spoken,
Expressed by one or more,
In solitude or in a group.
To communicate is to act upon words,
Being enlightened by the masses by a sedentary thought.
Being clear,
Being free to be you.
Words spoken,
Acted upon,
To give thought upon spoken words,
Thoughts left unsaid.

Dawn A. Campbell

Crazy Love

What kind of love affair are we having.
Is it faith or destiny that has brought us together,
Or is it just crazy love.

How can we continue this affair,
When I am not available,
And you are available to everyone you meet.

How can we allow this crazy love to continue.
You with your boyish ways and charming personality,
And I with the love of another.

How can this love go on.
How can you and I allow it to continue.
To continue,
We risk loosing everything,
Including our love.

However how strong,
Or how good it is,
We must risk loosing it,
Otherwise we might end up loosing ourselves and the ones we love.

You give me,
Love,
Love,
Love,
Crazy love.
Crazy,
But not madly deeply in love with you.

Dawn A. Campbell

Deeper and Deeper

Deeper and Deeper as I slip into a trance,
I find myself entranced by your wonderful vision.

Deeper and Deeper as I fall in love with you,
And you with me,
Thoughts of you become embedded in my mind.
My body wrapped up in your soul.

As I discover you,
You and I have become one,
Forming a comfortable union.
A union unstoppable by mere human contact,
Human envy and or greed.

Deeper and Deeper,
I am living a blissful life,
Falling deeper and deeper in love with you.

Dawn A. Campbell

Keep on Smiling

When life throws you a curve,
Nothing seems to be going right,
Keep on smiling.

When grave misfortune keeps coming your way,
When it seems like the world is caving in all around you,
Don't fret,
Don't despair,
Just keep on smiling.

Behind every cloud is a silver lining.
Smile and the whole world smiles with you.
Laugh and the whole world laughs with you.

When frustration starts to set in on a great day,
Have faith,
Keep smiling,
Cause sooner or later,
The clouds will open up,
Sending good fortune your way.

When your smiling,
Keep on smiling,
So that the whole world can smile back at you in return.

Dawn A. Campbell

Night Magic

Sitting by the waters edge holding hands,
You could see the shimmering shadows cast upon the water,
By the wonderful suplance of the moon.
The moon so bright that the light intensified the fire within,
To cause a catastrophic eruption of feelings waiting to be unleashed
upon any and all physical contact.
The appearance of stars made it a picture perfect affair.
Their presence was a blessing and a gift,
Which sent those hormones performing on overdrive,
Stirring a deep ceded magical bond.
This made them reluctant in giving up,
And little resistance in letting go.
The fire within burned even stronger,
When the brief encounter was over,
The fire was still there,
With the volcano waiting to erupt,
Even thought they both knew it would not happen tonight.
They both knew that the next time may not have such a short
ending.
The story will be even longer,
With the eruption of the volcano occurring not once,
But twice for the moon and the stars to see,
Sending a choir of music in the air.

Dawn A. Campbell

Passion of the Music

The passion I feel through the eye of the music,
Is wonderful and inspiring.

Though dysfunctional and chaotic at times,
It brings me to the land of the inevitable abyss.
It makes me feel inspired to create yet another musical melody,
Coming from of old to the present day.
Inspiration that is not conjured up or stored away.
Real feelings and emotions waiting to be released upon the world
and everyone in it.

To be inspired by an idea or a thought,
Encased in your mind, body and soul,
Just waiting, wanting to swallow you up,
Taking you to a place you have never been before except in your
dreams.

Dreams,
The reality maker,
The forgiver of all souls.
Your carrier to the next life.

To be inspired by the sound of the music,
Is to be inspired by everything that is real and tangible.
Grasping onto more than just a few straws and retaining every
ounce of dignity and pride,
While earning and getting respect,
Simply for the love of the music.

Dawn A. Campbell

The Magic Of Love

Who can understand the magic of love.
It comes at times when you least expect it,
Sending shivers down your spine,
Taking you back to wonderful times spent together,
And places you have been.

It's the feeling of love and happiness that brings
Two people together and let's them stay together.

True love never dies,
It lives on forever,
Until death does it part.

Dawn A. Campbell

The Shadow

Looking out my window,
I see a shadow that resembles you.
A shadow of immense feelings,
Dating back to the first time we met.
A shadow that holds many memories and unfulfilled dreams.
As the shadow comes closer,
I see a picture of you,
The one that my heart belonged to.
If only you could come closer,
Close enough to see tears of joy and sadness,
Rolling down my cheeks,
If only you were here, and not there.
If only you weren't just a shadow.

Dawn A. Campbell

Inspirational Quote

Even though I walk through the valley of the shadow of death,
I will fear no evil, for you are with me,
Your rod and your staff, they comfort me.
Psalms 24:4

No one knows why or how we are chosen when death is immanent around the corner. All we know, is that when our time comes, we have to surrender ourselves to the inevitable abyss of the graveyard shift. It is important to live each day to the fullest. Living each day as if it is your last. The choices you make in life is not often the right ones, but when your time comes, it is important to make peace with your maker and have no regrets about a life gone by or snuffed out before time.
Live life,
Love life,
And enjoy it to the fullest.

Dawn A. Campbell

A Broken Down Woman

Here lies the skeleton of a broken down woman,
A woman who has lost touch with reality before she died.
A woman who had totally given up on life.
She had no hopes for the future.
Her aspirations for the future were very slim.
The moral of her life,
Was nothing ventured,
Nothing gained.

Here lies the skeleton of a broken down woman.
A woman who has given,
Even when there was nothing left to give.
Her life has been a total disillusion,
Marred by blurred memory.

Now as we lay this dishevelled body to rest,
We praise the body by saying,
Ashes to ashes,
Dust to dust,
Let's say goodbye to this distant memory that was this broken down
woman.

Dawn A. Campbell

A Tragic Life

Like Machiavelli,
He predicted his death.
Death eminent around the corner,
Another rapper gone.
His meaningful life cut short before his time.
The drums are now beating faster to a different drummer.
When will it be his turn,
When will it be my turn,
To become one of the fallen heroes of our time,
The prince of his trade,
Bargaining his soul with the crypt keeper,
The guardian of his humanly remains.
Break the chain,
Stop the continuing cycle of yet another senseless killing.

Rapper by trade,
Gangster by choice,
Living the thug life.
You live by the sword,
So shall he die.

Life,
A precious commodity that we all take for granted.
We should all love and cherish it.
We should all be grateful for each and every day we are blessed with
it.

Dawn A. Campbell.

Childish Remains

My skin is full of nothing but withered flesh,
Separating from the bones of my body.
Once a man,
Then an adult,
Now reduced to a child like state again.
Instead of colored wrinkled flesh full of character,
You are reduced to the solemn destitute of a human being,
Waiting for nature to take it's course,
Sending you into the inevitable abyss of the grave yard shift,
Where you prepare to meet you maker,
The caretaker of your humanly remains.
The immortal life that existed before you got taken over by your soul
guardian is now over.
Your meagre existence begins.
Once a man,
Twice a child.
Child by nature,
Adult by choice.

Dawn A. Campbell

Deadly Bullets

Pop,
Pop,
Pop,
Goes the bullets from the gun,
Another one dead before time.

Dead before he could reach his next birthday.

You live the life,
So shall ye die by the life.

It is ironic that he predicted his death before it happened,
Recording his new self title album "Life After Death"
How dramatic of a life he lead.
Cut short before time.

What a blessing and a curse to foresee the future before it happens,
Lord have mercy on his soul.
A tragic soul.
A tragic life,
Cut short before it was able to develop into a grown man.

Dawn A. Campbell

Death Becomes Him

Yet another young life,
Cut short before time.
Like Machiavelli,
He predicted his bleak future
His life,
Cut short before he would realize he was grown.
A life rot with tremendous pain, guilt, trying to overcome many
adversities in his public controversial life.

Going through the struggles and daily grind of life,
Was more than just a mere struggle.
It was a matter of life and death,
Each day he was awaken to the phrase,
Thank you for yet another day.
Each night he would be grateful for making it this far.

The end is near,
The days getting shorter,
The nights non existent.
It's just a matter of time before the grim reaper finally sings his
song.
Pop!
Pop!
Pop!
Another one gets shot.
Another soul gunned down.
That's the tragic life of a gangster.
You live by the sword,
So shall you die by the sword.

Life,
A precious commodity that we should all love and cherish.

We should definitely not take it for granted.
We should all be grateful for each day that we are blessed with it.

Dawn A. Campbell

Dying for the Cause

In Flanders Field where the poppies grow,
We counted the crosses strewn atop of the graves of lives had, loved
and lost.

We live for our country,
And subsequently we are willing to die for it too,
All in an effort to serve and protect.
Bodies seen as martyr's,
Souls a distant memory in the eyes of the politicians and the com-
mon man.

Stop the bloodshed,
Stop the violence,
Another soldier gets shot.
Gunned down for the sake of peace, love and harmony.
A body bag escorted home,
With pomp and circumstance,
To soothe the heart and soul of a nation,
Given to a loved one.

In Flanders Field,
Here lies the bodies of a desolate few,
Fighting, loving and dying for the cause.
To serve and protect a nation, mankind and humanity.

Dawn A. Campbell

Dying Without Just Cause

In Flanders field where the poppies grow,
A testament to love had and lives lost,
Serving and dying for your country,
A living testament to achieving or not achieving success.
To return from the depth's of heaven or hell,
Showing little or no battle scars except the ones unseen by the naked
eye.
Graves marked or unmarked,
Serves as a monument to those who were willing or unwilling to
sacrifice their very existence for the country they serve.
No one knows when the torment will ever end.
No one knows when souls will stop being sacrificed ,
Only the desolate few,
The ones who hold the country in the palm of their hands,
And the souls of those lost.
Love had,
Lives lost,
Never to return,
Except in the mental crevices of our mind.

Dawn A. Campbell

Gone Too Soon

In the twinkling of an eye,
He was snuffed out before his time.
Breathed his last breath,
Sighed his last sigh.
Gone too soon.

An innocent life,
Taken at a time when there Is advanced medical technologies.
Taken all because of an unwillingness to seek medical attention.
Another life gone too soon.

Death has no boundaries,
Age no limitation.
Yet another life gone way too soon.
Only with a few fleeting last words.
Mommy I 'm coming home,
Home to where I belong.

* In memory of Leon.

Dawn A. Campbell

Inspirational Quote

"we also exult in our tribulations, knowing that tribulation brings about perseverance, and perseverance, prove character, and proven character hope; and hope does not disappoint, because the love of God has been poured out within our hearts..."
Romans 5:3-5

To persevere through all of life's challenges,
Is a living testament to having a higher power in our life.
Life's trials and tribulations are made easier,
Because he said he will never leave us nor forsake us. His glory and magnitude in our life is just the beginning of the journey on life's highway that he will take us through.
This life is but a test. We are literally living on borrowed time, so make the most of it, enjoy it, love it, and live it to the fullest, holding nothing back, yet taking nothing for granted.

Dawn A. Campbell

Don't Block Your Blessings

Don't block your blessings,
Don't try to control your own destiny.
Why tempt faith when you can put your trust in the Lord and allow
him to run it for you.
Why settle for Mr. Right Now,
When you can wait and have Mr. Permanent.
Why trust your judgement,
Thinking you are doing the right thing,
When you can have someone do the driving for you.
Life is so complex,
Full of ups and downs,
Ins and out.
A series of misfortunes giving way to heartache and disappointment.
Why tempt faith,
When you can put your trust in the preacher man,
Saving souls and giving life,
Leading you down life's vast highway.
Trust brings hope,
Which brings love.
Love yourself,
Trust in the Almighty Father,
And life will take you places you have never been.
He will take you to a life longing to have,
Desperately hoping to find,
Not knowing that it's a life already had,
Faith brings hope,
Which brings way,
To reality.

Life is a journey to live, love and experience to the fullest with no
regrets,

Of a life lived,
A life loved and enjoyed to the fullest at all times.

Dawn A. Campbell

Eternal Damnation

If your hungry he will feed you.
When your thirsty,
He said come to my well and take a sip of this sweet mountain honeydew.
Like turning water into wine,
And making the blind man see,
These are just a few of his mystical tricks called blessings.

Where can you go and buy wine and milk without money.
Where can you go and have your soul delivered and sanctified without just cause.
He said incline your ear and come unto me;
Hear and your soul shall live.
He will weather the storm raging in your life.
He will carry you through generational curses, divorce, sickness, health, joy and happiness,
All the while acknowledging that there are lessons to be learned through it all.

How slow the clock ticks upon the wall.
Oh how time seem to stand still,
Leaving you breathless, speechless and without words audible to mankind.
A language brought about through a séance of a tongue of old dialect,
Spoken in a foreign language not known by the carrier;
Speaking,
Talking,
Uttering words.
Mouthing lathing,
Spurting Chinese or Japanese,
To who knows or understands.

A language not known to the natural carrier.
Words conjured up as in a séance like state,
Looking,
Searching for others of the same faith,
Gathering strength,
picking up speed,
Yearning to disperse it on the intended target,
Not knowing that this is the day that the Lord has made.
Their souls will be connected,
Intertwined as one,
Speaking,
Singing,
Crying out the same tunes,
Chiming a melody,
Unknown but striking a familiar chord,
Recognizing that he is Lord El Shaddai Jesus the Almighty.
The saviour to every soul.
The elusive visitor of every dream,
Taking you beyond reality,
To the caretaker of your soul guardian,
The sustainers of life;
Till death shall you part from him,
In death if you are saved filled and santified,
He will take you on to your next life,
Your most important assignment,
Leading you into eternal damnation,
Where you will either roam in bondage,
Fulfilling the tasks of your alter ego Lucifer himself
Or roam free giving way to you ultimately seeing the light,
Taking you towards your resurrection of eternal life.
To choose the later is to tempt faith by taking matters into your own hand.
To believe is to accept the faith that life has dealt you,
And pray for health, strength and guidance to make it through and get through it to achieve true salvation,
Which is a blessed life through him,

Your one and only eternal father.
El Shaddai Jesus the Almighty,
Your one true and living God,
Leading you into victory through Christ Jesus.

Dawn A. Campbell

Giving Thanks

The Lord is good,
The Lord is great.
Let's celebrate his wondrous powers,
And his magnificent and magical ways he has touched our lives.

Let's celebrate by praising him,
In his holy name,
Giving thanks for what he has blessed upon us and the people around
us.

Give thanks and praise to the Almighty,
The King of Kings,
Lord of Lords,
And the ruler of all creation.

Let's say a prayer of thanks in his holy name.
Praise be to God,
Our eternal and spiritual father.
Praise be to thy holy name.
Amen.

Dawn A. Campbell

Growing in Gods Grace

I want you to take me deeper and deeper, higher and higher.
Let me grow sweet and sombre in your love and grace.
Make me wiser,
Through your precious holy word.
Let me continue to grow in your grace and understanding of it.
Let me continue to grow higher in your precious holy word,
Taking me to a higher place,
A sweeter place,
With you at the helm of the ship,
Steering me into an inevitable abyss of a relationship with you,
Watching you sit on your throne of grace,
Encouraging us,
To grow higher and sweeter in love with you forever and always.

Dawn A. Campbell

I Shall Rise

You will never amount to anything,
Those words cut like a sharp knife from a dull blade.
To have,
To hold,
To abort,
To keep.
Why oh why did you have me.
No words go unnoticed.
No words go unpunished.
Thy tears are in thy bottle Lord.
Whatever you sow,
So shall ye reap.
Honour thy mother and thy father.
How can you honour the respect that was not given to you.
How can you cherish the love you were never given.
You go through life with low self esteem,
Poor self image,
All from the lack of love.
To honour,
To love,
To respect,
Is to gain the trust of another.
How can you behold,
Or take hold of what was not given to you.
To refute,
To lay blame.
How can you blame,
When the apple does not fall far from the tree.
To earn respect,
Is to gain trust.
To acquire knowledge is to seek wisdom.
Growing strong and fearful of your heavenly father,

Nurturing you,
Holding you,
Protecting you from the demons within,
Allowing you to become whole.
To feel loved,
To feel worthy,
To become humane or should I say human.
How do I love thee let me count the ways.
Loving me is the only thing I dream of,
Because to love me, Is to love you.
Loving you is accepting the consequences of how I came into this
world.
To have,
To hold,
To keep,
To let go.
No matter how it goes,
I have to accept things as they are and move on.
Thy tears are in thy bottle Lord.
To have,
To hold.
Blessed be unto thee,
I shall rise,
I shall rise.
I shall be a star shining bright in the eyes of the Lord.
Like the star that shone brightly on the city of Bethlem.
I shall rise,
I shall rise.
Day comes,
But night catches up with it.
On the day of reckoning,
I shall rise.

Dawn A. Campbell

It's All In The Name

Whether you call him Jehovah Jireh, El Shaddai, Allah, Buddha, it does not matter,
As long as you praise him.
You bow down to him,
And most of all you respect and revere him.

It does not matter what umbrella you cover under,
As long as you are covered under the blood of Jesus Christ,
The blood of the lamb.

No matter who you pray to,
Or bow down to,
It does not matter as long as the Lord is on your side.

Through the good and the bad,
You will prevail because you are standing on the solid rock,
The solid rock of the Almighty Saviour.

Let him bless you as you bow down to him.
Let him lift you up as you pray to him daily,
Giving him offerings of thanks and praise.

The enemies and the evil doers have no say in your life.
They will not tarry,
They will not prevail because the mighty hand of Jesus is on your side.

Bless him and call him whatever you want,
As long as you continue to revere him and respect him all the way.

Bless him and praise him as he takes away all your fears and worries.

Cry to him,
Call to him,
Sing to him.
Through heavy burdens and crosses to bear,
The Lord will take it all away.
He will make a way out of no way.
He will provide for all your needs.
He will never leave you nor forsake you.
Never forget that we are not governed by the laws of this world.
We are governed by a higher power,
A higher authority.
Wherever there is a way,
He will surely make it for you.
He will take you deeper and deeper in love with him each and everyday.
Built him up,
Lift him up and he will continue to sustain you.
Blessing you with your heavenly rewards here on earth.

Dawn A. Campbell

Just A Walk With Thee

Come walk with the father,
And let him show you the way to true happiness and fulfilment.
He will lead you into a spiritual abyss that will not only be
enriching,
But fulfilling and rewarding to the soul with inner peace.

Dawn A. Campbell

Praising Him

Let's pay tribute to the most high,
Let's sing a song of praise in his honour.
Through the ups and downs of life,
He has been a constant figure in our lives,
Taking us through some of life's difficult challenges.
He has been there when friends have gone astray,
Given up on you and left you stranded.
He has been there when no one cared,
The boss was on your back,
Your co-workers trying to bring you down.
He has been the sustaining force through it all.
He has certainly helped you through the tough times as well as the good.
By the grace of God you manage to survive and continue striving through it all.
Stick with him,
And he will take you places you have never been.
What an awesome God you have,
When you can put your hand to the fire,
And pull it back,
He continues to love you still.
Through love,
Through strife,
He will never leave you nor forsake you.
He is truly our Rock of Gibraltar,
Our knight in shining armour,
No life has truly stood the test of time without him being a part of it all,
Sustaining you,
And most importantly giving you the ultimate gift,
The wondrous gift of life.

Life,
Love it,
Live it.
Enjoy it to the fullest,
With no regrets of a life had,
And a life lived well.

Dawn A. Campbell

Rise Above It

In a world rot with pain and suffering,
Only you know how to solve the everyday struggles of life.

They have done you wrong,
Done everything and anything to bring you down,
But each time you manage to rise above it.

They throw stones in the road to block off your destined path,
But you walk above it.
They put two paths instead of one,
Somehow you manage to follow your instinct and choose the right
one.
You rise above it.

Rise above it my friend,
Rise above it.
Every cloud has a silver lining,
Each time the sun rises,
Ye shall rise.
Through all the wrongs that have been dealt to you,
Ye shall rise.
Rise above it and become strong.
Become a leader not a follower.
Stand up and be counted.
Let your presence be known and felt in the world.
Rise up,
Stand up and be known.
Be known as a person instead of a number.
Rise above your dreams,
Make all your dreams become a reality,
So you can say,
I have risen,

Yes thank the Lord,
I have risen.

Dawn A. Campbell

The Sacred Cup

From the communion cup it overflows,
The nectar of the Gods,
Cleansing us of our impurities,
Saving us from our sins.
To drink,
To taste,
To eat the sacramental fruit,
Honing us home to our Master and Lord.
Let's give a toast,
To symbolize,
The cross,
To bow,
To pray,
Offering ourselves as sacrificial lambs unto thee.
Willingly,
Freely,
Hail to the king,
The most high God.
Allah to some,
Jesus to others.
As a symbol or a figure,
He is the source of life,
Fertility,
Strength and a source of perseverance to carry on.

Dawn A. Campbell

Worshipping Him

To have fellowship,
To worship the Almighty;
To come together in one accord.
Sitting down with Elijah, Peter, Paul and Abraham,
Discussing the sacred one,
Talking about his grace and his presence in our lives.

To hear the old melodies,
Mix with the hymns of today.
The sweet sensation of the rhythm of the dance,
Conjuring up the true undeniable worship hymns of old,
Bring our grandparents and our forefathers into play,
Giving us a distinctive essence of what it is to be in love with the
mighty deliver,
Giving him the love and respect he deserves through worshipping
and praising him,
Giving him shouts of thanks and praise through spiritual
utterance,
Praising him,
Worshiping him,
Thanking him for all and what he has blessed and given to us.

Your standing on the rock.
On the rock of solid ground is where you stand,
Praising him and worshiping him to the very end.

Dawn A. Campbell

Woman Of God

Being a woman of God,
Not a conceptualized woman of God.

To have and to hold,
Him near and dear to your heart.

To sing praises unto him,
Speaking as a kindred spirit from of old.
Captivating the audience of the Evangelical Faith.

Faith by any other name is just faith.
Faith, love and joy.
To have to hold,
To love him unconditionally without rhyme or reason.

Let's hail the one we call the Messiah,
The Almighty,
King of kings,
All hail the one true and living God.

Let's pay tribute to the holy one.
Hail Mary,
Hail to the Messiah,
The one true and living King.

Dawn A. Campbell

Patience In The Meantime

Patience for the meantime.
To wait on your word,
To wait on your timing
Full of the dream destroyers,
And pressures of all kind,
Waiting,
Wanting to take away all hopes for a bright future,
Robbing you of your earthly inheritance.

To have a dream,
To bear fruit,
To see your vision come to pass,
Only to have it taken away,
Without warning or without hesitation.

To live by Grace,
Is to live by faith.
Faith in the meantime,
Giving birth to patience.
Patience in knowing when to wait.
Having enough faith to wait on him for your ultimate deliverance,
Of your heavenly blessings here on earth.

Dawn A. Campbell

A Prayer Of A Thirsty Soul

Lord give me the Grace to survive another day.
Lord give me mercy to live on.

Correct me of my wrong doings,
Answer my pleading prayer.

Give me glory,
Give me satisfaction,
Learning to love you,
To be near to you.
Learning to trust you,
Unbelievable but true,
To find all hope in you.

Lord give me that captivating spirit,
In knowing that your love is so strong,
Showing the reason why you died on the cross.

Save my soul from condemnation,
By man and the world.

Give me strength to carry on,
To grow fervent in your love and your grace.
Allow me to continue to live in your grace,
Truly in my experience and understanding of it.

Help me to reach out to others as you have done to me.
Give me healing within my mind, body and soul.
Continue to be a blessing to me and to all and who I come in contact
with.
Help me to continue to motivate, incite and inspire continually.

In Jesus Name.
Amen.

Dawn A. Campbell

Grace And Mercy

Speak to my heart Blessed Holy Spirit.
Give me the word holy spirit,
That will encourage me,
That will give me life.
Leading me into victory through Christ Jesus.

I wish I know what you require of me.
I wish I knew what you wanted from me.
Desires of my heart unfulfilled to meet the needs of a demanding
world.

To work,
To write,
To create but a melody of my heart.

To uplift.
To inspire an imagined heart,
To beat the drum of a thousand drummer.

If only I knew your hearts desire.
If only I knew what you require of me,
To make it through yet another day.

If only I knew how to please you,
Not knowing that you were already pleased with me,
Through blessing me and lifting me up to tell the world of your
goodness and greatness in my life,
For to honour you,
Is to honour myself.
By your sights I am healed.
Through grace by faith I am alive and will continue living,

Living for your goodness,
Not my own.

Dawn A. Campbell

David's Dance

Learning on the light of his everlasting glory.
How I love to see the spirit dance.
Dance in the realm of a David Dance.
To capture a heart,
To capture a soul.

Loving the life,
Living the life loved.

Daniel in the Lion's den,
Fighting the dance of a thousand years.
Leaning on the past,
Looking towards the future,
Clinging to the present.

To dance a jubilee,
Mingling,
Paying respect like the nights of the round table.
Jesus with all of his disciples,
Singing chords of joy to the Angels.

Jesus is the rock on solid ground on which we stand,
Calling,
Crying out to thee,
Fleeing the realm of the David Dance,
To the dance of angels protecting thee.

To thee oh Lord I lift up my soul.
For unto thee a child is born,
To Mary and Joseph.
Stamped, sealed and delivered.
Set to make his mark on this world and life itself.

Jesus is the rock on solid ground on which we stand,
To have,
To hold.
To know him as our Lord and Saviour.

Knowing he will never leave you nor forsake you.
Lifting you up in his tender loving arms.
Loving you,
Carrying you,
As a keeper of your soul and your dreams.

The very essence of who you are.
Leaning on the everlasting arms of your saviour.
Tried and true,
I think I have found you.

Dawn A. Campbell

Inspirational Quote

It is good to give thanks to the Lord.
And to sing praises to your name, O Most High;
To declare your loving kindness in the morning
And your faithfulness by night.
With the ten-stringed flute and with the harp.
With resounding music upon the lyre.
For you, O Lord, have made me glad by what you have done.
I will sing for joy at the works of your hands.
How great are your works, O Lord!
Your thoughts are very deep.
Psalms 92:1-5

The most important gift we can ever attain in our life time, is the
gift of life. Nurture it, care for it, and it can last a long time.
Live life,
Love life,
Laugh a lot,
And enjoy it to the fullest.

Dawn A. Campbell

A Childs Hunger

Like a stalker,
Lurking through the night,
He probes my inner being,
Searching,
Wanting desperately to be held and comforted.

Like a loud siren,
He cries for attention,
Wailing and blasting the sounds of hunger.
The sounds deafening and piercing to the ears,
Only the sight of a mother can quiet this loud but hungry child.

Dawn A. Campbell

Convicted

To convict,
To lay blame.
Wrongfully convicted that's you.
Year after year you sit in that cell,
Thinking,
Contemplating,
Why oh why am I here.
Why was I convicted of this crime.
Taken away from my family in shackles and handcuff,
Brought in a court of law and proven guilty instead of innocent,
All based on the word of one.
I was chastised,
Brought forth,
Judged,
Tried and convicted,
Left for dead in this empty room called a cell.

Dawn A. Campbell

Hero

There is a hero in each and everyone of us.
We just have to look inside ourselves and seek it out.

We are born natural heroes.
It's what we do,
And how we do it,
That separates the men from the boys.

It's how we orchestrate a plan,
Begin to formulate a plan,
And turn it into something that makes us different.

It's how we market the finish product that matters,
That's what separates the winners from the losers.

Dawn A. Campbell

New Born

Oh sing out loud,
Oh sing the praises of a new day,
For unto us a son is born.

A beautiful baby boy,
Coming into uncharted territory.
Coming into this world as a blessing and a bearer of good tidings.

May we all sing the praises of his name.
May we all sing in the joy of his birth.

Hallujah! Hallujah! Hallujah Amen.
He has been delivered.
Delivered unto thee.
Praise be thy name.
In his honour,
Lets sing a song of joy.
Hallujah! Hallujah! Hallujah Amen.

Dawn A. Campbell

Paying Tribute

From Rosa Parks to Harriett Tubman,
History has defined the faces of the black man and woman.
Social consciousness,
Not just words,
But an inspiring belief among most of us.
Through segregation, slavery, apartheid and now separation.
How far have we come,
From the days of Dr. Martin Luther King.
How far have we come from the Sermon on the Mount,
How far have we come from the Civil Rights Movements and the
freedom marches.
To change lives,
To change a society rot with racial stereotypes of a time once was,
To a time that continues to be in certain places.
How far has life taken us,
How far will it take us,
To be free,
To see me,
To see you,
Living in unity instead of poverty,
Rising to the top of your stature,
Where no glass ceiling exist,
No differentiation between black and white.
Love has lost,
But has not lost at all in love and war.
To persevere through meagre existence,
A product of the times.
To make changes,
To change lives,
Making a difference on the world and man kind,
Making your mark,
Setting the stage for things to come.

Diary of a Poetic Mind

Making an impact on the nation.
Through strife comes integrity,
Perseverance begets excellence,
Striving for it,
Loving it,
Measuring yourself against it.
Stand tall,
Stay strong,
Take the message of the sixties into the twenth century,
Using the voices of the people.
Rosa Parks have now become Oprah Winfrey,
Dr. Martin Luther King have now become Senator Obama,
Giving life,
Breathing life unto a nation.
A nation of prosperity, love, peace and freedom.
Love the life you live,
Live the life you love,
Respecting and paying tribute to the people who paved the way for us,
To live the blessed life we now have,
And have now become accustomed to.

Dawn A. Campbell

Persecuted

Everyday we are persecuted,
Tried and convicted through the media,
From one human to another.
We are tried and tested everyday,
To attest to our faith,
Our true conviction.
How damming the case,
How strong the prosecution.
Shall it be heaven or hell.

Lets gather around to try the case of a sinner preaching conversion
to lost souls.
Lets convert the once sinner to a child of God.
All of your sins are now washed away,
Since you have been washed in the blood of the lamb.
You are now saved, filled and sanctified through Christ Jesus.
Get ready for your holy visitation,
To convert you from your earthly form to your new heavenly form'
Encased in the blood of the lamb,
To take control of your new found possession,
Free to worship,
Free to sing,
Free to preach the word of the Almighty Saviour.
Through him all things are possible.
As you continue your daily walk with him,
He governs your life.
He guards your going outs and coming in.
He captures every beat of your heat,
Like a love struck lover.
All praise to him,
Loving you,
Giving you life,

Lifting you up to all eternity.

Dawn A. Campbell

Stranger in a Promise Land

How I yearned for the days when I could come and visit.
A place where the days are short and the nights are long.
How I yearn to walk about the community,
Good morning,
Good evening,
Such as the case may be.
Looking back life was such fun,
Full of amazement and wonder,
Laughing gaily out loud,
At someone else's misfortune.
Now,
Coming into the same community does not hold the same sentiments.
I have become a stranger,
A foreigner in an unforgotten land,
Knowing more than before,
But now knowing nothing at all.
The quest towards the meaning of life,
Is but a dream,
A distant memory into the story book called life.
As I look towards the future,
There is great hope,
Looking forward to things to come,
Yet desperately ,
Hopelessly clinging unto the past.
Life holds significant memories,
Giving way to all of life's greatest rewards.
Rewards envisioned,
Not imagined.
Goals achieved,
Earned,
Preserved looking towards the future,

To all of life's greatest gift,
The gift of everlasting life.

Dawn A. Campbell

The Ghost of Mississippi Burning

Like a thief in the night,
They come to rob us,
Rob us of our dignity,
Our pride and self worth.
Like raiders they come to destroy us.
They come to trample upon us,
And run us into the ground.
They thought they were treating us like the slaves we were.

The masses have chosen to enslave us in eternal damnation,
Robbing us of our dignity and pride,
Trying to keep us down,
Trying to imprison us,
Like soldiers of our time,
Enlisted to fight in a war that didn't appreciate or cater to those
Negros.
Negros by name,
Blacks by color,
Proud by choice,
Cause through color comes distinction.

Dawn A. Campbell

The Rum Bar

Sitting in the Rum Bar,
Drinking Rum Bar,
A spirit contrived by man,
To rob the inner spirit of his blessed soul,
Evoking mental séances,
Wandering,
Traveling,
The mind does crazy things.
To learn on,
To hold on to the bar stool for support,
Lifting you up,
To carry you to your next pit stop,
To the next Rum Bar.

Dawn A. Campbell

War

The world,
Dominated by fear and ignorance.
Ruled by dictators and full of oppression.
A vision all too clear to us.

As the world suffers daily conflicts,
We seek refuge in the hands of man,
Who in turn rules for a settlement of scores,
Through human bloodshed and physical violence.

A world Roth with derogation and poverty,
Only the few will survive,
And the time has come.

Here you are looking at the few,
You and I.

They went over there as an army of proud soldiers,
And came back a desolate few,
Showing signs of post-mortem depression and a secret wish to die.
Their only dream,
Is to rid the world of the rulers,
So that their oppressors can finally have their day in court.

Dawn A. Campbell

Words

Words,
As empty and shallow as they are,
Their just words.
If you live in a glass house don't throw stones.
If you use hateful words,
Scars are sure to be left.
A constant reminder of the damage done.
No scars,
No wounds to tend to,
No cross to bear.
Nothing but a heavy laden burden.
Open up your eyes,
Pour out your heart,
Salvation is coming.
On that day of reckoning,
Show me your scars,
Show me your tears.
He lift me up.
He build me up,
Delivering me from the shadow of evil,
The perils of this earth.
Deliver me and lift me up dear Lord,
So that I can see true salvation.

Dawn A. Campbell

Wine~The Spirit Of Life

Red,
White,
Merlot,
What constitute a good wine.
Each begs to differ.

From a Sommelier's eye,
It's in the eye of the beholder.
To sniff,
To drink,
To enjoy the pleasure of,
The essence of,
The secret of,
For the love of,
The flavour of,
The mellow aromas.
From berries to earth to the tannins.
For the love of France, Australian, Chilean, Italian and South
African,
Each a cherished place.
Each a cherished flavour.
Aroma it's extreme content.

Red,
White,
I beg to differ.

The taste,
The many flavours,
The one and only everlasting taste of wine.

Shaken no.
Stirred not.
Just swish, taste and enjoy,
The simply admonishing taste of a breath taking flavour of a full
bodied gentle flavour that is wine.

Dawn A. Campbell

The Darker Brother

I am the darker brother.
Strong dark,
Not like the coloured brother.

Beat me up,
Turn me out,
I'm still the darker brother.

No sun can burn me.
No oil can hold me.
I will never burn.
I will never peel.

I am the darker, stronger brother.
Strong,
Buoyant,
Athletic and determined.
Darker not lighter.
Yes, I am big and strong.
Education a must,
Cause strong I am.
Light I cannot be,
To be free,
Like me.
The darker brother that's me.

Dawn A. Campbell

A World Gone Wrong

Looking into those eyes,
I can see those precious tears turning to blood.
Blood shedding with uncontrollable rage,
For those going off to war,
The million of starving children around the world.
We cry at the derogation of society and the role man has played in
it.

As I look forever into your eyes,
My thoughts hopes and dreams for tomorrow,
Become embedded in those sadden pools you call eyes.

Tears,
Tears,
Falling like the rain.
Tears,
Tears,
Only you know my pain.

Dawn A. Campbell

An Unjust World

Robbing from Peter to pay Paul.
What an unjust society we live in,
When most of us are living from hand to mouth,
While politicians and the designated few are living way above their
means,
Not giving a care of how the others live.

Millions living below the poverty line,
While the majority being just one pay check away.

How unjust is it that we have some driving expensive cars, eating
caviar and drinking the finest champagne,
While others are visiting the food bank,
Some fairing worse,
Not having anything to eat.
The hungry look of a child,
An undaunted thing to explain.
Where does the aid go,
Where does the charity donations disappear to,
Certainly not to the intended beneficiary.

Celebrities are only but a few championing the cause,
The poverty plight of the people.
Weather in the third world,
Or in our own backyard,
We are all a nation of one;
Yet in the western world,
It's everyman for themselves'
Everyone to their own order.

How can we go on.
How can we live with ourselves knowing that we are taking bread

Diary of a Poetic Mind

from someone else's mouth.
How can we not afford to take care of our people.
Politicians and servant leaders need to take charge,
Take the rains and help our people,
Instead of helping the rich get richer,
While the poor continues to fight the status quo,
Going against all odds,
Hoping that tonight is the night,
That their numbers will finally play.
Will it be for 6/49 or super 7,
No one knows,
Only you alone know what true faith lies ahead,
The controller of our destiny,
Which is the difference between survival and living a meagre existence.

We live in a world where the system is built up of dictators and oppressors,
Controlling the right to live and the right to die.
How can we morally justify the happening of a war that seems relentless without end.
If it was the basis of food and shelter we are fighting for,
It would have ended long ago.
There would be no unnecessary bloodshed,
No lives lost.
We should hope that the very essence of life would be worth fighting for.

How can we save our people from dying,
How can we spread the wealth,
So millions can enjoy some of it.
How can we encourage one another to give willingly form the heart.
Love your neighbour as yourself,
Give and the whole world will get in return.
Carry it forward,

So that the world can enjoy some of life's great pleasures,
Life's great gift and blessings,
Giving and tithing is the very essence of life.
The staff of life,
The great foundation of our generation.
Give and the whole world give with you.
Your store basket will be forever full,
Never empty.
Reach out with your heart,
Don't let the celebrities be but a few.
Reach out and let their be more,
Carrying on the torch for many generations,
Helping one another to make it,
To strive and survive throughout generations and life itself.

Dawn A. Campbell

Black and Proud

Say it loud,
I'm Black and proud.
Through strife,
Through tribulation,
Degradation,
We have arrived.
We have been beaten down,
Chained and shackled,
But we continue to persevere.
Through apartheid and segregation,
We manage to over come the odds.
Through the many names,
We have endured.
We have persevered through it all.
From the N word,
To coloured,
To black,
We have overcome the odds stacked against us,
And made it into the twenth century,
Living a life of love and happiness,
Going against the grain.
With the odds stacked against us,
We have integrated into our lives,
The very people that held us back,
Kept us down.
Now we are pioneers,
Success stories,
Leader of companies,
Head of organizations,
The word conglomerate our middle name.
Once scorned, beaten and blamed.
We have now risen above being a statistic,

Living on the system.
We have set the stage,
Living a life less ordinary.
Say it loud,
I'm black and proud.
Proud to be who I am and what I have become.
From the promise of a Dr. to living like a king,
We have certainly arrived,
Poised to take charge,
To own,
The right to be free.
Free to be who and what we want to be.

Dawn A. Campbell

Fight For your Rights

Rise up,
Stand up and be counted.
Stand up for your rights.
Fight for what you believe in.

Be seen,
And let your presence be known.
Let the whole world see you for who you are.
A leader among men,
A fighter till the bitter end,
Making sure your mark is left on society.
Making it known that you have beliefs.
It's for those belief that you are willing to lay your life on the line.
To die a violent death if necessary.
You live by the sword,
And if necessary you would die by it too.

Rise up and let your presence be felt.
Stand up and be counted as one.
Prepare to do battle with your public enemy number one,
Yourself.
Battling against a mind and body that has been ravaged by the ele-
ments of time.
Trying to bring back the essence of time and years gone by,
Is not so easily done or accomplished.
Be prepared to accept faith and life as it comes.
Accept the fact that you will have to do battle with your mind and
not your body.
In the end,
The mind always triumph over the body,
Leaving the body merciless,
Weak and decayed.

Ravaged by time and losing the right to become an individual,
Your public enemy number one,
Yourself.

Do not tempt faith,
Accept things as they are,
And you will soon reap the sweet rewards of the better sweet re-
wards of success in life,
My one and only you.

Dawn A. Campbell

Freedom Train

Toot, Toot,
All aboard,
Let's ride the freedom train.

Let's say a prayer for freedom.
A prayer for those who fought and died for this very cause.

Come one,
Come all,
Hop aboard on this historic event.
The very day we as a nation of blacks can stand up and be counted,
Fighting to stay out of the cotton fields,
And into the oval office.

From slavery to poverty to freedom,
Thank God,
For the very day when we can say I am free.

Freedom,
Freedom to change,
Freedom to live,
Freedom to love who we want.

Free at last,
Free at last.
Thank God almighty,
We are free at last.

Dawn A. Campbell

Generational Curse

Release the innocence,
Release the sublime,
The generational curse cuts like a knife.

From generation to generation,
The generational curse keeps on traveling.
From one sibling to the next,
Taking lives,
Taking souls,
Not allowing you to prosper.
Anger turns to hate,
Love turns to scorn.
Why does the hands of time keep going backwards.
Why does the hand of time momentarily seem non-existent.
Why does the curse seem to follow every generation,
Not letting go of the trend started.

How can the curse be broken.
When will it ever end.
When will you be the one to break the curse.
No one knows right now,
Only time will tell.

Dawn A. Campbell

Life

Tested tried and true,
We go through a series of emotions,
Through this up hill journey we call life.

Every breath I take,
Every though I make,
Has been made to uplift the mind body and soul.

Thought process hope to gain,
In solitude of a stance.
To make known the presence of another.
To gain the faith or strength of one.

Not knowing weather to laugh or cry,
Through life's up hill climb of mixed emotions.
A door closed is the answer to another one opening to support the
cause,
Casting a shadow of doubt but instilling faith to carry you through
with a silent whisper, taking you through life's journey,
A journey into the unknown.

Inevitable but true,
You have found you.
Don't know weather to laugh or cry.
Sadly but true,
You have found the true you.
The very essence of who you are,
Through the port holes of your mind.

Live it up,
Celebrate it,
This new found essence of who you really are.

Life is a journey,
Live it,
Love it,
Pass it on so others can enjoy it as much as you do.
Release the innocence of life's essence of the world.

Dawn A. Campbell

Words Left Unsaid

To speak,
To write,
Eloquently the two.

To know the heart of another.
To hear the voice,
Staccato words spoken as the status quo.
Keeping so close,
Dear to the heart of another love.

Love of my life
Where have you been.
Loving me,
Helping me,
Keeping me close.
Praise him,
Sing it out loud.
To phrase it,
To ask it,
The words won't flow free,
As the birds that fly free,
Flying to elude capture,
Capturing the heart of a life running,
Flying, beating fast.
Grab a hold unto it.

Staccato words spoken,
Unspoken a thought less spoken.
To give,
To live the life.
To be free as the bird flying,
Fleeing to elude capture.

Capture of the heart spurn,
To run free,
Be free as the wind blowing on the tree.

Words spoken unto me,
Words spoken to be free,
Set free,
Like me.

Dawn A. Campbell

Rhythm Of A Dance

To dance to the music,
To feel the beat,
The rhythm of the music inside of me.

To sing a lullaby,
To dance a jig,
A quick step or two.

To hug the body,
To love a tune.
How the music envelopes me,
Escapes me,
To keep me nourished and inspired.

To dance,
To live a life of love,
A life of happiness,
Dancing the dance of a thousand years.

How I love to feel you,
See you,
The music in me.
Keeping me a tuned to the world and connected to you.
The rhythm of my heart,
The beat of my soul.
The music an awe inspiring love of the dance
To dance,
To love,
To be free,
Free to be me.

Dawn A. Campbell

Determination

Your chains will never break me.
Your words will never tear me down.
A spirit of determination is what I have.
A soul that will never divide.

Luck be by my side,
Life love songs leading me on.

Through determination, self doubt, reservation,
No chains, no shackles will keep ,me from achieving striving for the
goals that matter to me.

Lead me on my blessed saviour.
I have great hope and faith in you.

I know you will never leave me nor forsake me.
Keeping me motivated,
Keeping me inspired.
I will not be defeated.
I will not back down.
I am strong,
I am wise.
I stand strong in the face of adversity.
Through faith, hope and the willingness to survive,
I will carry on.

Dawn A. Campbell

"Therefore I say to, all things for which you pray and ask, believe that you have received them, and they shall be granted you."
Mark 11:24

Life is a journey to be experienced, loved and enjoyed to the fullest. Continue to find inspiration in and around your surroundings. Always continue to challenge the status quo, going against the grain, following the road less travelled, always blazing a trail for yourself.
Be continually motivated, incited and inspired by all and what you do, by educating, empowering and enlightening not just yourself, but everyone around you.
Most importantly continue to be open to the possibilities of what can happen in life through living by faith by the power of prayer.

Seek ye first the kingdom of God and all that is his will be yours.

This might be the end of the book, but it is only just the beginning for me in this great and wonderful journey called life.
Life= LIVE IT FOR EVER, not your way, but his way.
Amen.

Dawn A. Campbell